THE LION
BIBLE
IN ITS
TIME

For Edward, Oliver, and Joseph   S.N.

Text by Lois Rock
Illustrations copyright © 2011 Steve Noon
This edition copyright © 2011 Lion Hudson

The moral rights of the author and illustrator
have been asserted

A Lion Children's Book
an imprint of
Lion Hudson plc
Wilkinson House, Jordan Hill Road,
Oxford OX2 8DR, England
www.lionhudson.com
ISBN 978 0 7459 6015 9

First edition 2011
10 9 8 7 6 5 4 3 2 1 0

Acknowledgments
Bible extracts are taken or adapted from the Good News Bible published by
the Bible Societies and HarperCollins Publishers, © American Bible Society
1994, used with permission.

A catalogue record for this book is available
from the British Library

Typeset in 12/15 Latin 725 BT
Printed in China June 2011 (manufacturer LH06)

Distributed by:
UK: Marston Book Services Ltd, PO Box 269, Abingdon, Oxon OX14 4YN
USA: Trafalgar Square Publishing, 814 N Franklin Street, Chicago, IL 60610
USA Christian Market: Kregel Publications, PO Box 2607, Grand Rapids, MI 49501

THE LION
BIBLE
IN ITS
TIME

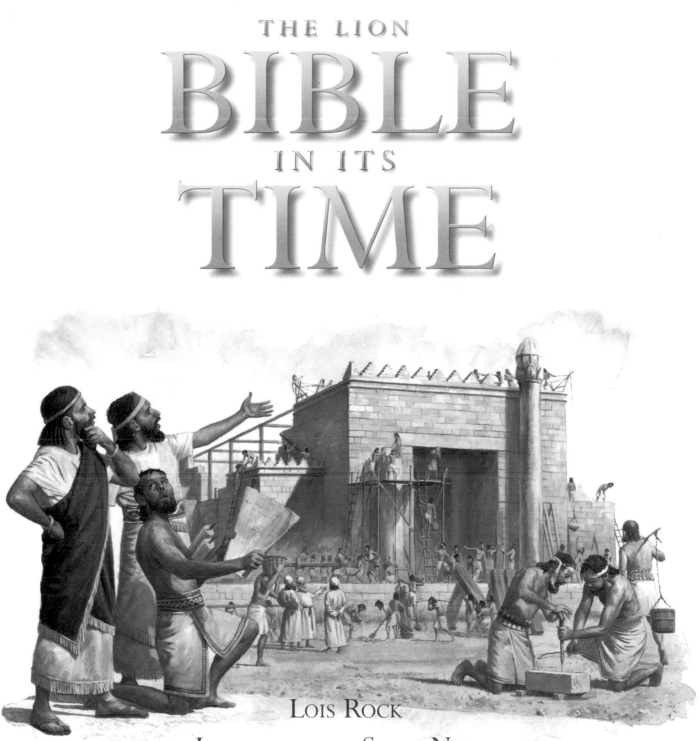

Lois Rock

Illustrated by Steve Noon

LION
CHILDREN'S

INTRODUCTION

The Bible is a world treasure. Because it has become so widely available in up-to-date language, it rarely causes much of a stir these days. Even so, it remains a hugely important collection of writings from the ancient Near East and is an astonishing window into times past. Among its collected books are several different types of writing including story, history, law, poetry, proverbs, and letters. The oldest of these writings may date back nearly 3,000 years. The most recent are not quite 2,000 years old.

The writings are also referred to as scriptures. As varied as they are, they are considered to be holy books, each in its own way giving insights into the great questions of why the world exists and what life is all about.

The older books are the scriptures of the Jewish faith. They tell of a God who made the world and who chose the Jewish nation to be a special people – obeying God's laws and showing the world what true righteousness really was. Time and again, they failed to live up to their calling. As the years went by, holy men known as prophets promised that one day God would send his chosen king to lead them in the right way. The word they used for chosen king was "messiah". A Greek word with the same meaning was "christ".

The more recent books tell of the one who was born a Jew and whose followers believed him to be the Christ. This man was Jesus and his followers became known as Christians. They claimed that Jesus' teachings showed people the right way to live. To this day, those who call themselves Christians treasure both parts of the Bible as Scripture.

All of the writings remain rooted in real history, and the purpose of this book is to bring that history to life. Through that lens it is possible to come to a better understanding of them: to learn about them and from them.

CONTENTS

IN THE BEGINNING

"Let there be light." According to the creation story, God spoke these words and the world began.

An ancient world view

The account of creation at the very start of the Bible says that in the beginning there was only a wild and chaotic nothingness like an ocean. God divided the waters of this primeval ocean so there could be earth, sea, and sky – and all living things – under the ocean of heaven. The storyteller may have imagined the cosmos like in the diagram here:

Heaven of Heavens

Ocean of Heaven

Firmament with the Stars

Pillars of Heaven

Earth

Underworld

Primeval Ocean

Pillars of Earth

The first book in the Bible is called Genesis. The word itself means "beginning", and the book contains stories about how the world came to be the way it is. The origins of these stories are lost in the mists of time: their words were passed on as stories told aloud long before they were written down.

Even so, the stories are set firmly in the real and recognizable world of the ancient Near East.

Creation stories

The Bible begins with a creation story. It is a poem that tells of God making the world in six days – the earth, the sky, the sea, and everything in them. On the seventh day, God and all creation rested. This pattern of six days of work and a sabbath day of rest became a law of living for the Bible people, the Jews.

The second story in the Bible is about the Garden of Eden. God made it to be a paradise home for Adam and Eve – the first man and woman. They disobeyed God by eating fruit from a forbidden tree. In this way, evil entered God's good world.

Farmers and shepherds

After they had disobeyed God, the story goes, Adam and Eve had to leave the Garden of Eden. In the harsh world they found, they had to toil for a living. Their eldest son, Cain, became a farmer and grew crops. His brother, Abel, became a shepherd. Cain was jealous when God seemed to favour Abel. In fury, he murdered Abel, and for this God told him he would bear the consequences.

The story reflects the way that ancient peoples were learning to make their living in the fertile lands of the region (shown in green on the map). It is also told to show God's view of human quarrelling.

Cain was a farmer; his brother Abel was a shepherd.

A flood and a world made new

The Bible book of Genesis speaks of many generations going by. In all those years, it says, wickedness spread over the world. God planned to end it in a great flood and begin the world afresh. God chose the one good man, Noah, to build a floating ark on which a pair of every living creature would be safe.

The story of Noah has striking similarities with another ancient story from the same region: the epic of Gilgamesh tells of how a hero-king by that name built a boat to save his people and animals.

For the people of the Bible, however, the story of the disastrous flood and the world's recovery from it pointed to one thing: the world belonged to God. The rainbow that spread across the sky after the rain showed God's promise to care for the world for ever.

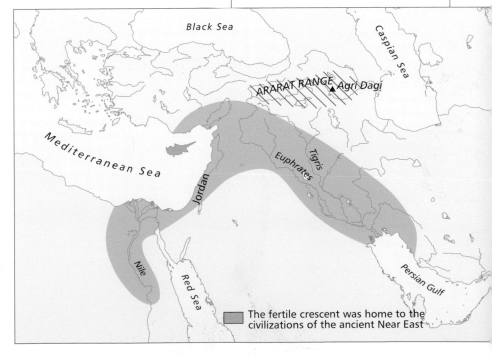

The fertile crescent was home to the civilizations of the ancient Near East

THE GREAT FLOOD

The story of Noah and the flood appears to be set on the plain between the rivers Tigris and Euphrates. These rivers rose among mountains far to the north. When the snows melted in spring, the rivers flooded and left fertile soil on the plain. The ancient civilization of Sumer flourished on this productive land. Yet, from time to time, more disastrous floods could easily occur and threatened all living things.

City and temple tower

A leopard hunts its prey

Reed house

Soldiers

Bitumen pit

Animal-skin float

Guffa

Bitumen makes a
boat waterproof

Growing vegetables

Herding flocks

9

Abraham: Father of a Nation

The temple-tower of Ur

The city of Ur, the biblical birthplace of Abraham, is a site that has been rediscovered. Spectacular among the remains is a temple-tower, or ziggurat, built for the worship of the moon god Nannar, some 4,000 years old.

In its day, such a building, made of local brick and bitumen, was a triumph of technology. However, it fell to ruin.

The Bible story of the tower of Babel, or Babylon, is about a people who thought they could build a tower so tall and magnificent that they would be as great as the creator God. However, as the tower rose higher, God caused them to speak different languages. They were unable to understand one another and could no longer work together. Instead, they went off to find new places to make their home, leaving the tower unfinished.

The ziggurat at Ur is the setting that hearers of the story might have called to mind.

The story of the Bible centres on the story of one nation: the people of Israel, later known as the Jews. The book of Genesis tells stories about the beginning of that nation and a man named Abram, later changed to Abraham: "father of many".

Abram sets out

Abram was born in the city of Ur. It had been a wealthy and important city from around 2500 BCE. His father took the family to Haran. The Bible says that when Abram was seventy-five years old, God told him to take his family and go in search of a new land where he could make his home: Canaan. God also promised that he would become the father of a great nation.

The builders of a ziggurat like this may well have thought that their technological skills would enable them to rule the world.

Abram took his flocks and herds to begin the life of a nomad, always on the move in search of pastures. His family grew wealthy. The time came when he and his nephew, Lot, decided it was wise to divide the household.

However, Abram's wife, Sarah, remained childless. As was the custom, she gave Abram her servant, Hagar, to bear him a child – a son she named Ishmael. But God had promised to bless the family of Abram and Sarah. At last, they had a son, Isaac.

One day, the Bible says, God told Abram (now Abraham) to offer Isaac as a sacrifice. Abraham took his son to a mountain top, built an altar there and tied him up, ready to kill him. At the last moment, God told Abraham to stop. He had, the story says, proved his obedience. Although the story is puzzling, Abraham became famous among his descendants as someone of very great faith.

Sodom and Gomorrah

Abram's nephew Lot took his family to settle in the region of two cities near the Dead Sea, Sodom and Gomorrah. According to the Bible, their inhabitants lived such wicked and immoral lives that God sent a storm of sulphur to punish them. Lot escaped, but his wife turned back and died, encrusted with salt.

Dramatic salt formations near the ancient site of Sodom and Gomorrah. Because water can only escape the landlocked Dead Sea by evaporation, the dissolved mineral salts in it are very concentrated. The fringes of the sea are a natural salt pan.

ABRAHAM: A NOMAD IN CANAAN

Abraham's household consisted of his wife, Sarah, and his servants and their families. Their flocks provided them with meat, milk, wool, and leather. They were able to trade some of these goods with the local Canaanite farmers, who grew crops including grain, olives for oil, and grapes for wine.

Travellers from different ethnic origins used the trading routes between the civilizations of Mesopotamia to the north and Egypt to the south.

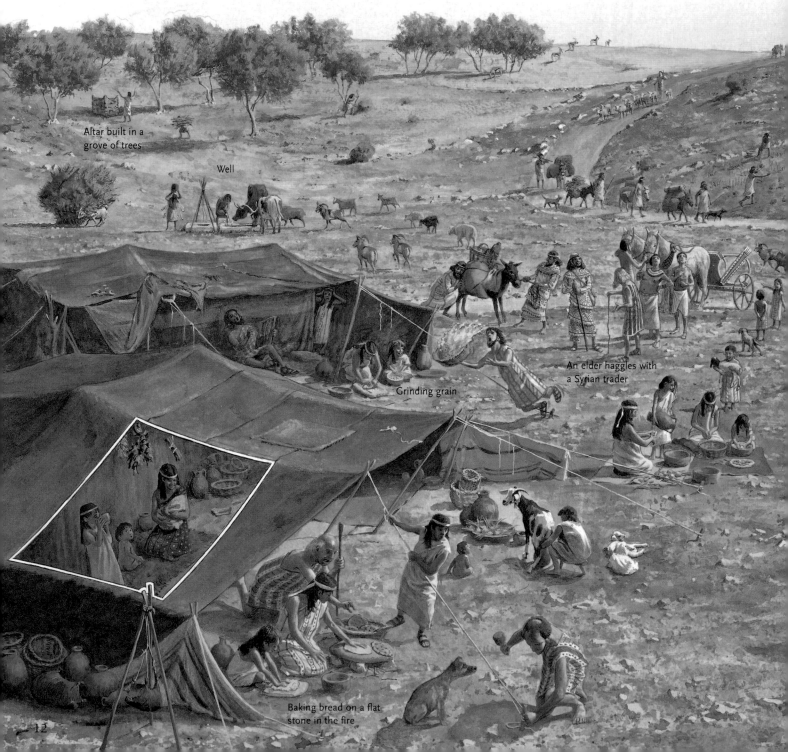

Altar built in a grove of trees

Well

Grinding grain

An elder haggles with a Syrian trader

Baking bread on a flat stone in the fire

Walled Canaanite city

Tents of goatskin and
canvas for the nomadic life

Local Canaanites trade
farm produce

A hammock cradle

A slave girl argues
with her mistress

Sheep's wool and goat hair
are dyed, spun, and woven

JACOB AND HIS FAMILY

The people of Israel

When Jacob journeyed home from where Laban lived to Canaan, he met a stranger who challenged him to a fight. The struggle lasted all night, and in the dawn light Jacob understood that he had been fighting with God. The stranger gave him a new name to mark the event: Israel. Jacob had twelve sons, and from them emerged twelve great families: the twelve tribes of Israel.

Joseph's special coat might have been a multi-coloured cloak like this.

When Abraham grew old, he was anxious that his son Isaac should not marry a Canaanite. He asked a trusted servant to travel north to find a wife for Isaac from among his relatives. The servant's journey was so successful that he believed God had blessed him and helped him to find the right woman: Rebecca. The young woman's brother, Laban, agreed that she should go and be Isaac's bride.

Esau and Jacob

Isaac and Rebecca had twin sons. Esau was the elder of the two. He was a strong huntsman and Isaac admired him. However, Jacob was Rebecca's favourite. Jacob was jealous of his older brother and, with his mother's help, schemed to win for himself the rights and privileges due to the firstborn.

Esau was furious at being cheated, and Jacob had to flee for his life. He headed north and offered to work for his uncle Laban. The older man tried to squeeze as much work from his nephew as he could for little reward, and the misery of being cheated changed Jacob. After many years, he returned to Canaan rather wiser.

He had worked hard for the wealth he now had: flocks of his own, two of Laban's daughters as wives – the plainer Leah and the beautiful and dearly loved Rachel – and a large household. Jacob's brother Esau had also prospered. The two made peace with each other and agreed where each should settle.

Joseph

Jacob had twelve sons, but his favourites were those born to Rachel: Joseph and Benjamin. Joseph was the elder, and one day Jacob gave him a wonderful brightly dyed coat. It was a clear sign that he was the privileged son.

The ten elder brothers were jealous. The more Joseph boasted of dreams in which his family bowed down to him, the more they hated him. One day, when Jacob sent Joseph to find out if the ten were looking after the flocks properly, they seized him and threatened him. They ended up selling him as a slave to traders on their way to Egypt.

As a slave, Joseph found out what it was like to have no privileges. In spite of his hard work, he was thrown into prison because someone told lies about him. However, he believed that God had given him wisdom to explain dreams, and people grew to respect him.

A harvesting scene based on a wall painting from ancient Egypt.

One day, he was hauled from prison to explain a dream puzzling the pharaoh, the king of Egypt. Joseph understood that the dream predicted seven years of good harvests and seven of famine. The king put Joseph in charge of storing food for the lean years.

During the famine, his ten brothers came to buy food for the family. They bowed to their brother Joseph, not knowing it was him. Joseph schemed for them to fetch his true brother, Benjamin. In the end, he forgave them all and invited his family to Egypt.

Egypt

Egypt was one of the wealthiest civilizations of the ancient world. Its rulers, the pharaohs, displayed their riches proudly. One of the great status symbols was the chariot.

The Bible says that the pharaoh rewarded Joseph for his wisdom by allowing him to use his second chariot. It was a sign of the respect that everyone who saw it should give him.

An Egyptian wall painting. In this period, chariot wheels had six spokes.

THE PEOPLE OF ISRAEL IN EGYPT

In Egypt, Jacob's descendants enjoyed the benefits of living in a rich and fertile land for many years. However, the reason for them being in a foreign land was forgotten. A new pharaoh came to power who ordered that they join the ranks of slaves.

Grain store

Official in a chariot

Vegetable plots

Laundry basket

Shaduf and irrigation channel

Cows are fattened on the lush riverside pasture

One of the pharaoh's magnificent building projects

Slaves making bricks from mud and straw

Cutting papyrus

Catching wildfowl

A princess on a royal barge

MOSES

The baby in the basket

According to the Bible story, Moses was the son of an Israelite woman who saved her son from the king's soldiers. They were under orders to find any baby boys and throw them in the river to drown them.

One mother made a basket to be a floating cradle and hid her child among the reeds. She left her daughter Miriam to watch. When an Egyptian princess came to that spot to bathe, she found the baby and had pity on him. Miriam said she could find someone to nurse the baby – and brought her mother. The princess raised Moses as her adopted son.

Papyrus sedge was a valuable resource, used for "paper" and in basketry.

This illustration of a brickfield is based on a painting from ancient Egypt. It shows the cruelty of the overseers.

Four hundred years of prosperity in Egypt came to an end. The pharaoh, who feared the people of Israel, made them his slaves. They had to make bricks for his grandiose building projects.

The bricks were made from mud and straw. When the Israelites complained about the work and the cruel conditions, the pharaoh stopped supplying straw so they had to work even harder fetching their own.

He also gave the order that all the baby boys born to Israelite women be thrown in the river. However, one mother found a way to save her son, who became known as Moses. When he grew up, he was dismayed to discover how his people were treated.

His first attempt at justice went badly wrong. He started a fight with a slave-driver, who was beating an Israelite, and killed him. In fear of his own life, he fled to the land of Midian and became a shepherd.

One day, alone in the desert, he saw a bush that appeared to be on fire but was not burning. From the burning bush, he believed he heard God speaking to him, telling him to go and lead his people to freedom.

Moses went with his brother Aaron to ask the pharaoh to let the people of Israel go. The king refused, even when one disaster followed another. Then, one night, death struck

One of the disasters that struck Egypt was a plague of frogs. Moses claimed these disasters were God's warning.

every Egyptian household, and he changed his mind. The Israelites remembered that night as Passover – when death passed over them.

The pharaoh ordered the people of Israel to leave. However, when they reached the shore of an inland sea, they saw that the Egyptian army had been sent to capture them. By a miracle, the wind blew a pathway through the water for them. The army was drowned. The people of Israel were on their way back to the land of their ancestors: the land of Canaan.

This story is found in the second book of the Bible, Exodus. The word itself means "coming out" and refers to the escape from Egypt. Traders and travellers often made the journey from Egypt to Canaan in days. However, according to the Bible, once the Israelites had escaped Egypt they spent forty years in the wilderness region in between. There they learned to trust in God to take care of them. God helped Moses find clean drinking water. Flocks of quails provided unexpected food. The people were able to collect the sweet, white flakes of manna from the ground in the mornings – a food that they regarded as miraculous.

Moses and the covenant

The Bible book of Exodus tells of Moses reminding the people of Israel of their relationship with God. One day, when they were in the wilderness between Egypt and Canaan, Moses went to the top of a mountain, Mount Sinai.

There, in the stillness, he wrote down the laws that God gave him. They were at the heart of an agreement between God and the people – a covenant.

Some of the laws were about worshipping God and God alone. Other laws were about being kind and fair to everyone.

According to the covenant, the people would obey God's laws, and God would bless them and take care of them.

THROUGH THE WILDERNESS

The direct trade routes from Egypt to Canaan were only a couple of weeks' journey. The people of Israel spent many years wandering the wilderness before daring to invade.

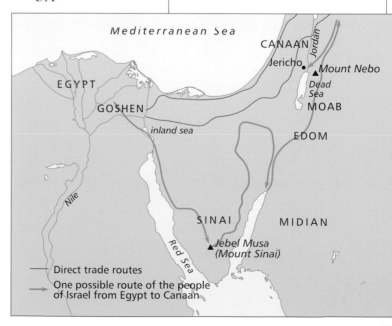

THE TABERNACLE IN THE WILDERNESS

During the time that the Israelites were in the wilderness, God gave the people laws through his prophet, Moses. These included laws about worship, and there were also detailed instructions for how to build a portable place of worship – a tent, or tabernacle.

In the innermost room, the ark of the covenant was kept safe. The tabernacle itself became the visible sign of the people's belief that God – their God – was with them.

Ox carts

Altar

Outer court

High priest and heralds

20

Quail

Golden lampstand

Holy place

Ark of the covenant in the Holy of Holies

Table of showbread

Incense altar

Bronze basin for washing

Young warriors with grapes from Canaan

Weaver

Goldsmith

21

CLAIMING THE LAND

The battle of Jericho

When Joshua led the invasion of Canaan, the people came first to the ancient walled city of Jericho. Once a day, for six days, the fighting men marched around. Some of the priests carried the ark of the covenant and others sounded the trumpets. On the seventh day, the procession marched around seven times. Then, when the priests gave a loud blast on the trumpets, all the people gave a mighty shout. The walls collapsed and the fighters took the city.

The story of Joshua is of a miracle, but beneath present-day Jericho is clear evidence of an ancient walled city.

Moses did not lead the people of Israel into Canaan. Instead, he glimpsed the land and all its promise from a mountain on the other side of the River Jordan, and there he died.

He had already chosen one of the young warriors who had spied out the land to be the new leader. This was Joshua.

Joshua believed that God enabled him to capture all of Canaan and give each of the great families of Israel a place to settle. When he grew old, Joshua gathered the people together and asked them if they would be faithful to God. "We will serve the Lord," they declared.

Champions of the people

However, it was hard to make a living. Even in a fertile land, no one could be sure of a good harvest. The people of Israel found it tempting to show respect for the local gods – including Baal, the god of the weather and fertility, and his consort, the goddess Asherah.

Such practices did them no good. Other nations were eager to raid their goods and capture their land. Time and again, they cried out to their own God for help. When they showed they were sorry for being faithless, says the Bible, God sent champions, called judges, to help them.

The stories of the judges are puzzlingly brutal. Among them is the account of Gideon, who believed God called him to lead a night-time ambush on the camp of the raiding Midianites. Even more violent is the tale of Samson, who led a one-man campaign of arson, murder, and mayhem against the Philistines.

The Midianites rode camels when they came raiding.

This carving shows Philistine warriors in their distinctive plumed helmets.

These were desperate times. The Philistines finally captured Samson when his lover, Delilah, betrayed him and the secret of his strength: his uncut hair, the sign of his being dedicated to God.

The Philistines hacked off Samson's hair and made him their prisoner. Some time later, they brought him to one of their temple festivals to mock him. The Bible story tells that his hair had begun to grow. Once again trusting in God, Samson tore down the pair of pillars that supported the roof, crushing himself and his people's enemies.

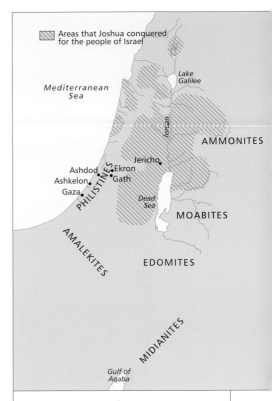

UNDER ATTACK

The Israelites had many enemies when they made their home in the land of Canaan.

A wise prophet

Through this time of unrest, the tabernacle stood at a place called Shiloh. A childless woman named Hannah went there for a festival and prayed that she would have a baby. When her prayer was answered, she dedicated her child to God and asked the ageing priest Eli to train him as a helper. The child – Samuel – became a wise leader who called the people back to worshipping God and obeying the laws. While he had charge, the nation enjoyed a measure of peace.

The boy Samuel

Samuel's mother arranged that he be a helper in the tabernacle at Shiloh, in the care of the priest Eli. One night, when Samuel was sleeping in the shrine, he heard someone call his name. He ran to Eli, but the old man said he had not called. This happened a second time and a third. Then Eli knew: it must be God who was calling the boy.

God told Samuel that Eli's sons had proved themselves unworthy to take on the role their father had performed. God had chosen Samuel instead.

FARMING THE LAND

In spite of many difficulties, the people of Israel made their home in Canaan, and farmed the land.

Beating olives from the tree

Harvesting wheat

The rooftop provides living space

Gleaning leftover grain

The pillared courtyard provides shelter for animals

Drying fruit in the sun

Watchtower overlooking
the vineyard

Gathering grapes

Treading grapes
for wine

Winnowing

Threshing barley with
a sledge

THE GREAT KINGS OF ISRAEL

Philistines

The Philistines were the long-time enemies of the people of Israel. By the time of David, they had the advantage of better weapons, having mastered the art of working iron to a sharp blade while the people of Israel relied on the softer bronze.

Their champion Goliath is described in the Bible as having fearsome weapons. David, the shepherd boy, had only the slingshot that he used to lob stones at wild animals who came to raid his flocks.

David claimed that it was because of God that he was able to secure the victory.

As the prophet Samuel grew older, the people of Israel became anxious about who would lead them next. They pleaded with Samuel to choose a king who would lead their battles against the plundering nations around them.

Saul

The first king Samuel anointed for the task was Saul – a strong and handsome farmer's son and a natural warrior. He won some great victories but he quarrelled bitterly with Samuel. The prophet accused the young king of making wilful mistakes, and for these, God had rejected him. God would not allow Saul's son to succeed him.

David

Samuel then asked God to show him who should be the next king. The choice fell on a young shepherd boy from Bethlehem: David.

The young man knew that he should not be king at once. However, he became the people's hero when he defeated the Philistines in a test fight against their champion Goliath. His popularity made Saul jealous, and in the end David had to flee for his life. He spent many years as an outlaw, hunted and hated. Even so, he remained a national hero, and other young warriors came to join him.

When Saul and his son Jonathan died in battle, David claimed the throne, dismissing rival claims. He then went on to lead the nation to victory over its enemies. David chose a hilltop fort to be his capital city, Jerusalem, and had the ark of the covenant brought there in a triumphant procession. However, he was not able to realize his dream of building a temple to house it.

David's slingstone caused the heavily armed Philistine champion to fall.

Solomon used the finest marble, cedar, and gold to build a Temple in Jerusalem.

Solomon

The young King Solomon prayed to God for wisdom and became famous for his judgments. He had inherited a wealthy kingdom and spared no expense in building the Temple his father David had planned – a permanent building to replace the tabernacle.

However, he grew fond of luxury, building a splendid palace for himself and his increasing number of foreign wives. He paid less and less attention to obeying God's laws or taking care of his people.

SOLOMON'S TRADE

Solomon's ships traded in the Mediterranean and in the Red Sea, providing him with many high-value items. Solomon also gained great wealth from taxing traders who used his land routes.

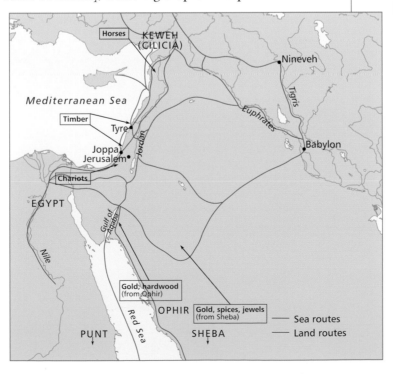

Horses
KEWEH (CILICIA)
Nineveh
Mediterranean Sea
Timber
Tyre
Jordan
Tigris
Euphrates
Joppa
Jerusalem
Babylon
Chariots
EGYPT
Gulf of Aqaba
Nile
Gold, hardwood (from Ophir)
Gold, spices, jewels (from Sheba)
OPHIR
PUNT
Red Sea
SHEBA
—— Sea routes
—— Land routes

Psalms and Proverbs

The time of David and Solomon is remembered as a golden age in Israel's culture.

David had been a great musician since he was a boy, and he wrote and sang songs: praising God, lamenting disasters, asking for God's help and God's forgiveness. Some of the great songs in the Bible – the Psalms – are credited to David.

Solomon was famed as a scholar who studied the world around him – plants, animals, birds, reptiles, and fish. He is also said to have written proverbs, or wise sayings, and other books of wisdom now in the Bible: Proverbs, Ecclesiastes, and the Song of Songs.

JERUSALEM IN THE REIGN OF KING SOLOMON

Solomon's Jerusalem was a splendid city. On the highest point was the Temple, modelled on the tabernacle but built of stone, fine wood, and precious gold. It became the national place of worship, with elaborate ceremonies.

Nearby was the royal palace where Solomon lived in luxury with his many wives.

The queen of Sheba, far to the south, heard of Solomon's wealth and wisdom and came bearing rich gifts to see if it were true. She was more than impressed.

Hall of the Forest of Lebanon

Gold shields

A queen enjoys the shade

Ornamental pool

The queen of Sheba

Children's games

Bathroom

Temple

Twin pillars
Jachin and Boaz

Chariot regiment

Court musicians

Schoolroom

Pet apes

29

THE DIVIDED KINGDOM

Queen Jezebel

A famous character from the kingdom of Israel was Jezebel, Ahab's foreign queen. She became a byword for wickedness. The story is told that Ahab wanted to buy a vineyard from a man named Naboth so that he could have an extra garden. Naboth refused, saying God's laws allowed him to keep his own land. Jezebel schemed to have Naboth falsely accused and executed. She then gave his land to Ahab.

After Ahab's death, when a young soldier named Jehu led a coup against the royal family, Jezebel's own servants threw her out of the palace window to her death.

Jezebel watches Jehu arrive, knowing he has come to challenge her.

King Solomon's projects were costly. He made his people pay high taxes and do forced labour. When he died and his son Rehoboam became king, people hoped for better times. However, Rehoboam was young and arrogant, and he threatened to make even heavier demands. Only the tribes of Judah and Benjamin stayed loyal. Their southern territory became the kingdom called Judah.

The ten northern tribes rebelled. They chose their own king, a man named Jeroboam. His kingdom was often referred to as the kingdom of Israel. It began around 930 BCE.

Israel and the broken promise

One problem for the northern kingdom of Israel was that the Temple was in Jerusalem, in Judah. King Jeroboam built shrines at Dan and Bethel as places of worship. In each he placed a statue of a golden calf. When the Bible writers looked back on the sad history of Israel, they marked this as the moment when the people broke the covenant with God.

Faithless kings

Soon after, a king named Omri came to power. He made Samaria his capital, and his son Ahab lived in luxury in the palace there. Ahab's foreign wife, Jezebel, worshipped a god named Baal and had no respect for God's laws. She encouraged her husband to act as selfishly as he liked. Under his rule, the people also lost their respect for God's laws.

As the years went by, there were some kings in Israel who respected and obeyed the God of their people, but more who did not.

THE DIVIDED KINGDOM

The northern kingdom of Israel was to be annihilated by the Assyrians.

Jehu and the tribute

Jehu was a young soldier whom Elisha chose to seize power from Ahab's corrupt royal family and the notorious Queen Jezebel. He was successful in his campaign and got rid of the worship of the foreign god Baal. Sadly, he later forgot about God and the kingdom slipped back into faithlessness.

During his reign, he had to give gifts to Assyria in return for not being invaded. An Assyrian obelisk depicts him bowing before the emperor Shalmaneser III. The writing reads:

The tribute of Jehu, son of Omri: I received from him silver, gold, a golden bowl, a golden vase with pointed bottom, golden tumblers, golden buckets, tin, a staff for a king [and] spears.

Jehu bows low to the Assyrian emperor. This carving, on a panel of a Black Obelisk, is the only known depiction of a named Israelite from the Bible.

Loyal prophets

The Bible tells of important prophets who did their best to remind the people of Israel to respect their own God. In the time of Ahab, the prophet Elijah risked his life to speak out against Ahab's wickedness and to demonstrate God's power to work miracles. When he grew old, he handed the same responsibility on to a younger prophet named Elisha, who also became famous in Israel for working miracles, even healing an enemy general, Naaman, a Syrian.

Later, another prophet, named Amos, was a shepherd from Tekoa in Judah. He railed against the people of Samaria who lived in luxurious mansions but didn't care about the poor.

Defeat

Meanwhile, to the north, the armies of Assyria had been conquering an empire. Disaster came in 722 BCE, when a man called Hoshea was king of Israel. The Assyrian emperor Shalmaneser V invaded Israel. The capital city of Samaria was destroyed and the people sent to other parts of the empire. The Bible says this happened because the Israelites were unfaithful to God.

DEFEATED BY ASSYRIA

It was around 720 BCE that the Assyrians swept down from the north and defeated the kingdom of Israel, destroying it utterly.

They also fought their way further south to Judah. One of the cities of Judah they captured was Lachish. The victory was an important one and the story of the battle was recorded on carved panels for the Assyrian palace – a carving on which this picture is based.

Siege ladders

A fire is lit to weaken the walls' foundations

Elaborately built enemy camp

Archers

The Assyrian emperor Sennacherib watching the battle

Male captives are brutally treated

Defenders hurl
firebrands

A siege machine with
a battering ram

Slinger

Straw shield

Women and children are
taken captive

THE KINGDOM OF JUDAH

The little kingdom of Judah fared better than the northern kingdom of Israel. One reason was that, for the most part, people accepted that descendants of David's family should rule there – whereas in Israel there had been a number of plots from those who wanted to take the throne.

A promise of a king

Even though the kingdom of Judah housed Jerusalem and its Temple, the people were not particularly faithful to God. Just as in Israel the prophet Amos had warned the people of Samaria about enjoying luxury but neglecting justice, so the prophet Isaiah warned the people of Jerusalem.

   The women, Isaiah said, gave all their attention to jewellery, clothes, and perfume. They were going to lose everything. The people loved drinking to excess, but they didn't care about the poor. "You are doomed," he told them. But he also said that one day God would send a king like David to set them free: a king of peace.

Hezekiah defends Jerusalem

As the Assyrian empire grew more powerful, Judah found itself facing the same invasion that had wiped out Israel. The Assyrian army captured several of the important cities of Judah. It swept on to Jerusalem and laid siege to it.

The water-supply tunnel under Jerusalem was cut in solid rock.

The siege of Jerusalem

King Hezekiah of Judah foresaw the dangers of the Assyrian invasion. He prepared for a siege in Jerusalem by ensuring the city would have water. He arranged for a tunnel to be made so that a spring outside the walls would feed a well inside. There was great rejoicing when the two teams of tunnellers met, having been guided by the sound of the other's hacking of the rock.

   This tunnel still exists.

This clay prism is covered with incised writing. In it, Sennacherib says that he has Jerusalem trapped "like a bird in a cage".

Confident of victory, the Assyrian emperor Sennacherib sent officials to demand Jerusalem's surrender. But then, mysteriously, death swept through the Assyrian camp and the army went home. The people of Jerusalem believed this to be a miracle.

Good King Josiah

Even though the people of Jerusalem had every reason to believe that God had helped them survive the Assyrian attack, they soon slid back into ungodly ways. Some time later, a boy named Josiah was proclaimed the rightful king when he was just eight years old. He was given good advice to help him learn how to be king, and he ruled well. When he was older, the Temple officials rediscovered the book of God's laws. Josiah called the people back to obedience to these laws. He forbade worship of other gods and held a great Passover festival.

Babylon

The kings that came after Josiah did not follow his example. They became caught up in the politics of the day: the Assyrian empire had given way to that of Babylon. A prophet named Jeremiah warned Judah to accept defeat but the kings rejected his message as too pessimistic. Sadly he was proved right, and in 604 BCE the Babylonians became the effective rulers of Judah.

Many of the people of Judah were led away to exile in Babylon.

King Hezekiah tried to prevent the Assyrian emperor Sennacherib from attacking Jerusalem. He sent gold and silver tribute from the Temple.

The ark of the covenant

After years of political intrigue between the kings of Judah and their overlords, the Babylonian emperor Nebuchadnezzar captured Jerusalem and burned the Temple down. This happened in 586 BCE.

The greatest treasure in the Temple was the ark of the covenant – the symbol of the promise made between God and the descendants of Abraham, and the place where the great laws the people believed God had given in the time of Moses were kept. It vanished in the destruction.

The whereabouts of the lost ark remain a mystery that has intrigued generations since.

The ark of the covenant was a golden box with two winged creatures on the lid. It was fitted with carrying poles and was considered too holy to touch.

BABYLON AND THE JEWS

It was in faraway Babylon that the people of Israel became known as the Jews –
a name that has remained ever since. Although the Babylonians had gods and temples,
the Jews had no place of worship.

Instead, they would meet as a community to keep their faith and their traditions.
This meeting became known as a synagogue.

The great North Gate is dedicated to the goddess Ishtar

City walls

A statue of the god Marduk is carried in procession

A statue of the god Marduk is carried in procession

The emperor Nebuchadnezzar

Processional Way

The Etemenanki, or
ziggurat, of Babylon

Heralds

Musicians

Jews refuse to
worship the
Babylonian god

Bridge over river

37

A CHANGING WORLD

A glimpse of part of the royal palace of Persepolis at the height of Persia's imperial power.

Tales from Babylon

The Bible book of Daniel tells of three young Jews resisting the orders of King Nebuchadnezzar. He wanted everyone to bow to a gold statue of the great god of Babylon, but Shadrach, Meshach, and Abednego said that they would worship only God.

The three young men were thrown into a fiery furnace. They were praising God even as they faced their terrible punishment. Then God sent an angel to protect them. Nebuchadnezzar set them free, praising them and their God.

Another story says that King Belshazzar of Babylon was enjoying a banquet and drinking wine from the gold cups looted from Jerusalem's temple. Mysterious writing appeared on the wall. A Jew named Daniel was summoned to read it: the words foretold the end of the Babylonian empire.

The defeat of the kingdom of Judah and the exile that followed might have spelled the end of the nation. In fact, it seemed to motivate the Jews to treasure their culture and their faith. More and more they turned to the ancient writings of their people – including the laws of Moses. They listened to the words of prophets from days gone by and to prophets of their own time, such as Ezekiel, whose sayings would later become part of their collection of Scripture.

Babylon and Persia

However, the period of Babylonian rule did not last long. After little more than sixty years after the fall of Jerusalem, the Medes and Persians defeated the Babylonians. The new rulers made a very important announcement: the Jews who lived in exile were to be allowed to return to Jerusalem and rebuild their Temple.

Rebuilding

Many Jews (though far from all) made the journey home. The rebuilding took several years, and even so the result was not nearly as splendid as Solomon's Temple had been. Later, a man named Nehemiah helped organize the rebuilding of the city walls, in spite of angry opposition from the people who had made their home in the old kingdom of Judah during the exile. Around this time, a priest named Ezra worked hard to make sure everyone knew the ancient laws that were at the heart of the Jewish faith.

Babylonian musicians practise for the New Year festival, when statues of the gods would be led out in procession.

Daniel expected to be killed in the den of lions – a terrifying form of execution.

The Greek empire

Within a century, there were more upheavals. A Greek general named Alexander the Great defeated the Persian empire and conquered lands beyond. He wanted all his conquered people to adopt the culture of Greece, and so did his rulers after him. They tried to force the Jews to give up their faith and their worship. In the end, a Jewish fighter named Judas Maccabaeus led a rebellion. He threw the altars and statues to pagan gods out of the Temple and rededicated it to God.

The Romans

For a while, the Jewish people had their own kings, but they were never truly free from the interference of more powerful nations around them. Since 499 BCE Rome had been the centre of growing military power, and gradually the Romans had been establishing an empire of their own. In 63 BCE the Roman general Pompey took Jerusalem.

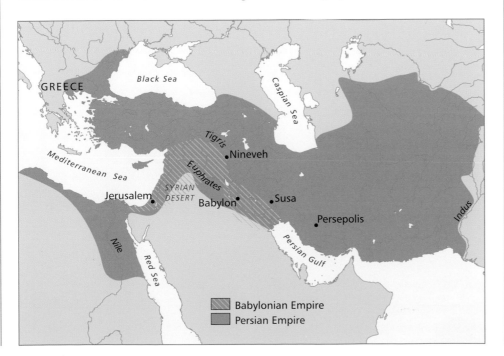

Babylonian Empire
Persian Empire

Tales from Persia

The Jews were still in exile from their homeland when Babylon fell to new rulers – the Medes and Persians. The story goes that the new king, Darius, chose the Jew named Daniel for an important job. Daniel's rivals schemed to have him thrown into a pit of lions for saying his prayers. God sent an angel to keep Daniel safe, greatly impressing Darius.

The Bible book of Esther is set in the heart of the Persian empire, in the royal palace at Susa. It tells how a Jewish girl named Esther was chosen to be a wife for the emperor. When an official named Haman schemed for the Jews to be massacred, she risked her life by asking the king to let them defend themselves.

CHANGING EMPIRES

The Assyrian empire, ruled from Nineveh, gave way to the Babylonian empire. This was in turn defeated by the Persians, whose empire extended east to nearly present-day Pakistan beyond the Indus and west to present-day Greece. Alexander the Great later defeated all this territory.

ROMAN JERUSALEM

The Romans needed local rulers to take care of the provinces of their empire, and in 40 BCE the title of "King of the Jews" was given to an ambitious and ruthless man named Herod. He himself was not a Jew by birth, but he tried to make the Jewish leaders accept him by undertaking to rebuild the Temple in Jerusalem.

Court of Israel

Court of the Gentiles

Animals for sacrifice

Moneychanger

Temple guard

Market

Roman garrison –
the Antonia fortress

Temple

Giant lampstands

Court of prayer

Court of the priests

Treadmill crane

High priest

Foreign legionaries

King Herod

41

JESUS IS BORN

Fields slope down from the hilltop town of Bethlehem.

Luke's story

Luke's Gospel tells one story of Jesus' birth: an angel appeared to a young woman in Nazareth, Mary, and told her she had been chosen to be the mother of God's own Son.

Some months later, the pregnant Mary went to Bethlehem with her husband-to-be, Joseph. It was Joseph's hometown and famous as the birthplace of King David. They had to go there to register as taxpayers. The guest rooms were all full, and Mary's baby, Jesus, was born in an animal room.

That same night, shepherds were out on the hillside with their flocks. Angels appeared and told them that the promised king, the Christ, had been born in Bethlehem and was cradled in a manger. The shepherds went to find the child.

By the time of the Roman empire, the Jewish people were longing for another great king. Since the time of the Babylonians, they had been ordered around by one superpower after another. Yet the Jews still believed they were a people special to God. Through war and in defeat, their prophets had foretold good news: God would one day send a king like David to rescue them.

Messiah, Christ

Then, when the Jewish territory was just a minor province of the Roman empire, a young man began preaching: Jesus. What he said and what he did convinced many that he was the promised king. The word for king in Hebrew was "messiah"; in Greek, it was "christ".

Jesus' followers became convinced he was the messiah and the Son of God. The stories of his birth pay tribute to that belief. These stories are found in two of the four accounts of Jesus' life now in the Bible – the Gospels of Matthew and Luke. The historical setting is clearly stated. Augustus is emperor in Rome, Quirinius is governor of Syria, and Herod rules on behalf of the Romans as king in Jerusalem. These clues set the date somewhere between 6 and 4 BCE – a little earlier than the Western calendar marks the birth of Jesus.

People line up at a Roman booth to register their names as taxpayers of the empire. This scene evokes what Bethlehem may have looked like at the time when, according to Luke, Mary and Joseph went to Bethlehem for this purpose.

King Herod had used every cruel stratagem to gain power and keep it. He would have been furious at news of a newborn king.

Matthew's story

Matthew's Gospel points out how the events of Jesus' birth matched what the prophets had foretold about the messiah's birth. For one thing, his family line went back to King David. For another, his mother, Mary, was a virgin and her pregnancy a miracle of God's Holy Spirit. Third, Mary and her husband-to-be were in Bethlehem when the child was born.

Matthew's Gospel tells that mysterious visitors arrived from the East. They had seen a star that they believed marked the birth of a king of the Jews. The star led them to Bethlehem, where they brought the child their gifts of gold, frankincense, and myrrh.

Jesus' baptism

By the time Jesus was a young man, another preacher had already made a name for himself. He was a relative of Jesus named John. He lived an unusual life alone in the desert and preached a fierce message to all who passed by: they must turn their lives around and live in obedience to God. Those who accepted his teaching he baptized, dipping them in the River Jordan as the sign of their new beginning. Some wondered if John was the messiah, but he said he was not.

One day, Jesus came asking to be baptized. As John lifted Jesus out of the water, he heard a voice from heaven saying, "This is my Son." He saw a dove settle on Jesus' head – a sign of God's Holy Spirit.

After he was baptized, Jesus went and spent forty days alone in the wilderness thinking of what lay ahead. The Bible says the devil came and tempted him to choose an easier way than preaching the message he believed God had given him. Jesus refused. The Jewish scriptures he knew so well helped him choose between good and evil.

Jesus asked his cousin John to baptize him in the River Jordan.

43

NAZARETH

Jesus grew up in the town of Nazareth. He would have learned to read and write at the synagogue school so that, as a young man, he could take his turn reading from the scriptures.

He would also have learned the family trade, as a carpenter and builder.

Sheepfold

Blacksmith

Basketmaker

Potter

Carpenter's workshop

Well

Oven

Spinning

Synagogue

Rabbi

Synagogue school

Beggar

JESUS THE PREACHER

Some sayings of Jesus

"Love your enemies and pray for those who persecute you, so that you may become the children of your Father in heaven."
Matthew 5:44–45

"If you forgive others the wrongs they have done to you, your Father in heaven will also forgive you."
Matthew 6:14

"Do not store up riches for yourselves here on earth… Instead, store up riches for yourselves in heaven… You cannot serve both God and money."
Matthew 6:19, 20, 24

"Do for others what you want them to do for you: this is the meaning of the Law of Moses and of the teachings of the prophets."
Matthew 7:12

John was a young fisherman when he became a follower of Jesus.

Jesus sometimes taught in the synagogues and sometimes outdoors, where large crowds gathered to hear him. This view is from a hill overlooking Lake Galilee, where Jesus is said to have preached.

Once Jesus had made the decision to become a preacher, he began to visit the synagogues in the surrounding areas. Many people found his message captivating, and he was often given a warm welcome.

The people of Nazareth, with whom he had grown up, were less convinced about the young man they knew as the son of Joseph. When it was his turn to read from the scriptures in their synagogue, and he hinted that he was God's chosen one, they turned against him. Indeed, they would have lynched him if he had not quietly slipped away.

In Capernaum

Jesus left Nazareth and the hills of Galilee for a fishing port named Capernaum, on the shores of Lake Galilee. Jesus had made friends with some of the fishermen there. Now he called four of them to leave their nets and become his full-time disciples. They were Simon (whom Jesus named Peter – "the rock") and his brother Andrew, as well as James and his brother John. Jesus went on to gather a band of twelve disciples in all, and there were many other people who supported him in his work.

Friends and followers

Jesus' message was all about God's love and forgiveness and how to live members of God's kingdom. Sometimes he preached directly; other times he told stories with a deeper meaning – parables.

In the court of prayer, in the Temple, one man proclaims his good deeds; another repents of his wrongdoing.

Miracles

The Bible accounts of Jesus' life all report that he worked many miracles. Everywhere Jesus went, he became famous as a healer. People reported that with just a touch or even a word Jesus could enable those who were lame to walk again. People with dreaded diseases were made well; blind people had their sight restored. Many people were eager for Jesus to help them or their friends. The religious leaders fretted about whether the power Jesus had could really be from God.

A parable

This story that Jesus told gave a strong message of what it meant to live as God's people should.

"Two men went to the Temple to pray. One was very religious, devoted to the Jewish law, a member of the group known as the Pharisees. The other was a tax collector, who made a fine profit from working for the occupying Romans.

"The Pharisee stood apart. 'I thank you, God,' he said, 'that I am not greedy, dishonest, or an adulterer, as others are. I thank you that I'm not like that tax collector. I strive to keep all the rules.'

"Meanwhile the tax collector stood at a distance and bowed his head. 'God have pity on me, a sinner,' was his simple and desperate prayer."

Jesus explained the meaning of the story: only the tax collector had seen the truth about himself. God would forgive him and welcome him as a friend.

Friends and enemies

Many people warmed to Jesus' inclusive message. They grew into an enthusiastic following, including many who were outcasts in society. Unsurprisingly, the religious leaders were not pleased.

PLACES JESUS KNEW

From his base in Capernaum, Jesus travelled widely within Galilee. His fishermen disciples were able to take him by boat to various lakeside towns and villages. On occasion he went further: in the northern town of Caesarea Philippi, the disciple Peter declared Jesus to be "the Christ". In Jerusalem, Jesus faced the anger of the religious teachers who rejected his teaching.

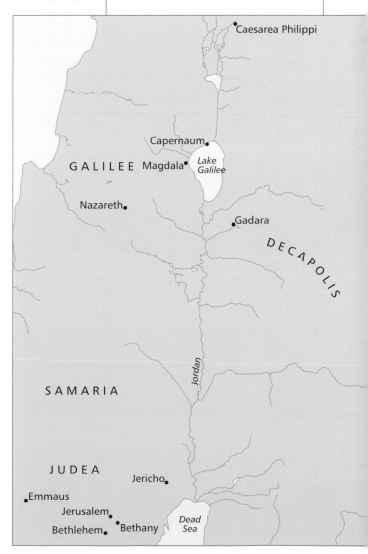

CAPERNAUM IN THE TIME OF JESUS

The lakeside town of Capernaum was where Jesus made his home after he was forced to leave Nazareth.

Jesus

Cast net

Boats working as a pair gather the catch from a vertical net

Washing clothes

Freshly caught fish

Watering cattle

Olive press

Flour mill

Broadcast sowing in a
ploughed field

49

THE CRUCIFIXION OF JESUS

Jesus' teaching was centred on the two great laws at the heart of the Jewish faith: "Love the Lord your God with all your heart, with all your soul, with all your strength, and with all your mind.... Love your neighbour as you love yourself."

However, the religious teachers were worried that Jesus was misleading the people with his message of forgiveness. They were concerned that he was upsetting their authority. They began to conspire about the best way to get rid of him.

Riding to Jerusalem

After three years, Jesus and his disciples came to Jerusalem for the Passover festival. He stayed with friends in Bethany before asking his disciples to fetch a donkey so he could ride into Jerusalem. Pilgrims on the road gave him a noisy welcome: they waved branches and shouted, "God save the king!"

Jesus made no claim to be king. He simply went to the Temple courtyard. The festival fair was in full swing. Some traders were selling animals for the festival sacrifices; others were exchanging everyday money for the Temple coins needed for the festival offering. Jesus was furious. "The Temple is meant to be a house of prayer," he cried. "You have made it a den of thieves." Amid great commotion, he threw them out.

The crown of thorns that Jesus' executioners crammed on his head was to mock the charge against him – that he was a king.

King of the Jews

When Pilate gave the order for Jesus to be crucified, he handed him over to his soldiers to conduct the execution. They first bullied him and mocked him, cramming a crown of twisted thorns on his head, draping him in a cloth of royal hue and beating him.

Following Roman practice, a notice of Jesus' "crime" was pinned to the cross. Pilate wrote in Latin, Greek, and Hebrew: "Jesus of Nazareth, the King of the Jews." The Latin words, "Iesus Nazarenus, Rex Iudaeorum", give the INRI often seen in pictures.

The Last Supper

The time came for Jesus to enjoy the festival meal and its traditional foods with his disciples. "This is my body," he declared as he broke the bread. As he passed his disciples he cup of wine he said, "This is my blood, poured out for many." Already he knew that one of his disciples – Judas Iscariot – was no longer loyal. When Judas left the room, the other disciples assumed he was on some ordinary errand. Jesus knew that Judas was going to betray him.

Arrested and condemned

Jesus and eleven loyal disciples went to spend the night in an olive grove. The garden of Gethsemane was just outside the city, at the foot of the Mount of Olives. There, in the dark, Jesus prayed for God to spare him what lay ahead… but it was not to be. Judas returned, bringing with him armed officers.

They hustled him off to be questioned by the religious council in the high priest's palace. They wanted to know if he claimed to be the messiah. Jesus refused to answer their question directly, so they declared him guilty. The crime they alleged was blasphemy – treating God with contempt.

The next morning, a Friday, they took him to be sentenced. A Roman governor was in charge of Judea by this time – Pontius Pilate – and he was not interested in religious matters. Jesus' accusers tried to persuade him that Jesus was claiming to be king of the Jews and therefore a threat to Roman rule.

Pilate remained unconvinced. However, a mob gathered outside the fortress where he sat in judgment, demanding that Jesus be put to death. Pilate did not want a riot, so he gave the order. The death penalty was crucifixion.

A body would be wrapped and placed in a tomb cut into the rock, sealed with a rolling door.

Jesus sent two disciples – Peter and John – to prepare a room for the festival meal he wanted to share with them. It is likely they would have eaten in the Roman style, reclining on couches around a table.

The death of Jesus

The Gospel of Luke records that, as he hung dying on the cross, Jesus prayed to God to forgive his enemies.

When it was clear that Jesus was dead, a wealthy man named Joseph, who came from Arimathea, asked Pilate for permission to take Jesus' body for burial. It was laid in a rock-cut tomb. The stone door was rolled shut and soldiers ordered to stand guard.

JERUSALEM IN THE TIME OF PILATE

The Jerusalem where Jesus was crucified was a religious centre for the Jews and an administrative centre for the Romans, who ruled it as part of their empire.

   The Temple that Herod had commissioned rose above the skyline. Next to it was the Roman garrison, the Antonia fortress.

The governor, Pontius Pilate

City wall

Soldiers dice for their prisoner's cloak

Antonia fortress

Temple

Preparing the ground for
the upright of a cross

53

THE NEWS ABOUT JESUS

The risen Jesus

The Gospel of John gives this account of the risen Jesus. A young woman named Mary Magdalene, whom Jesus had healed, stayed by the open tomb, weeping. Then she looked in the tomb and saw two angels, dressed in white. "Why are you crying?" they asked her.

"They have taken the body of Jesus away," she explained, "and I don't know where he is."

Then she turned around. She saw a man and thought he was the one who tended the olive grove. "Did you move the body?" she asked.

The man simply said, "Mary."

It was then that she recognized him: it was Jesus.

Jesus was crucified on a Friday, just before the sabbath day of rest. There was little time then to perform the usual burial rituals. After the sabbath, very early on Sunday morning, some of the women who had been followers of Jesus went back with the spices that were traditionally included when the corpse was wrapped. To their astonishment, the stone door to the tomb was open. There was no corpse inside.

The women who saw Jesus' empty tomb rushed to tell the other disciples. Shortly after, the Gospels say, Jesus appeared to his followers. Once they saw him, they were convinced: by a miracle, God had raised Jesus to life.

The great commission

Then one day, Jesus told his followers that the work he had begun was now theirs to continue: his instruction is known as the great commission. They were to be apostles – sent out to spread his message to the ends of the earth. As he spoke, a cloud hid him from their sight: they believed he had ascended to heaven. This event, the Bible says, took place forty days after the resurrection.

Pentecost

The disciples remained afraid for their own safety, but Jesus had promised that God would strengthen them with his Holy Spirit. Ten days later, during the Jewish harvest festival called Pentecost, they were meeting secretly in a room in Jerusalem. All at once they heard a noise like wind and saw tongues of fire leaping among them. Emboldened, they rushed outside to tell the news. Pilgrims from all over the empire had come to Jerusalem for Pentecost. They were amazed to hear Jesus' followers telling them about Jesus in their own languages. Peter stood up and addressed the crowd – and that day many became believers.

Persecution

Many people believed the disciples' message, and swiftly the religious authorities began harassing them. A promising young leader named Stephen was stoned to death. This persecution drove the believers elsewhere. One zealous young Jew was determined not to let them escape. His name was Paul, and he had stood by approving when Stephen had been killed. He went and asked for permission to go and arrest the followers of the Way of the Lord in a town miles to the north: Damascus.

A dramatic conversion

As Paul was travelling to hunt down believers, he was blinded by a mysterious light. As he fell to the ground, he believed he heard Jesus speaking to him. Paul's companions led him to Damascus. There he did indeed meet the believers: one of them restored Paul's sight and convinced him of the truth of Jesus' teaching.

The disciple Peter believed that God's spirit gave him the courage to preach about Jesus and his message. His first sermon was to the people of Jerusalem, including many pilgrims from different countries who had come for the festival of Pentecost.

THE NEWS SPREADS

As the numbers of believers in Jerusalem grew, the authorities there turned against them. The disciples then began to spread the message in other places, shown here.

Peter

Jesus' disciple Simon, renamed Peter, had always been bold and outspoken. On the day of Pentecost, he stood up in the middle of Jerusalem and preached about Jesus. He would not let himself be stopped by threats from the authorities.

After the death of Stephen, the disciples scattered. Philip went to Ashdod, where he baptized an Ethiopian as a follower. Peter went to Lydda and then Joppa. There, in a vision, he came to see that the message about Jesus was also for non-Jews – Gentiles. When messengers arrived from Caesarea asking Peter to come and preach to a god-fearing Roman officer named Cornelius, he went. Cornelius's entire household became followers of the Way of the Lord.

THE PORT OF CAESAREA

The port town of Caesarea was an important part of the network of shipping routes criss-crossing the sea at the heart of the Roman empire – the sea known today as the Mediterranean. Peter preached to a Roman officer stationed here. The apostle Paul arrived in Caesarea when he returned from two of his missionary journeys, and it was from here that he set sail for Rome.

Sailing boat

Prisoners

A galley with many oars

The home of a
military officer

Amphorae

PAUL'S MISSIONARY JOURNEYS

As a young Jewish scholar, Paul had been determined to stamp out belief in Jesus. When he himself became a believer, a Christian, he worked tirelessly to spread the news about Jesus.

He made use of the excellent roads and shipping routes of the Roman empire to visit places far beyond those that Jesus had known. He became convinced that the teachings of Jesus were as important for non-Jews as for Jews. He used his learning to help people understand his own beliefs: that Jesus' life and teaching were the fulfilment of the Jewish faith.

His travels were full of adventure. Sometimes he was welcomed and was able to establish a group of Christians – a church – who could help and encourage one another. Other times he encountered considerable anger and hostility. Some of this came from Jews who did not like him preaching to Gentiles. Some was from Gentiles who did not like the way his teaching upset their way of life. In Philippi he healed a young woman whose mental state made her useful as a fortune-teller. When her Roman owners realized she was no longer able to make money for them, they had Paul flung into prison. In the town of Ephesus the silversmiths who sold silver models of the goddess Diana to pilgrims and tourists rioted against him. In each case, Paul believed God was not only helping him survive but giving him opportunities to preach.

Paul dictated letters to a scribe. He said he had poor handwriting.

From Paul's letters to the people of Corinth

"Love is patient and kind; it is not jealous or conceited or proud; love is not ill-mannered or selfish or irritable; love does not keep a record of wrongs; love is not happy with evil, but is happy with the truth. Love never gives up; and its faith, hope, and patience never fail.

"Love is eternal.... Our gifts of knowledge and of inspired messages are only partial; but when what is perfect comes, then what is partial will disappear.

"Meanwhile these three remain: faith, hope, and love; and the greatest of these is love."
1 Corinthians 13:4–7, 8–10, 13

The Roman theatre at Ephesus. Although this building is later than the time of Paul, it evokes the setting in which Paul faced an angry mob.

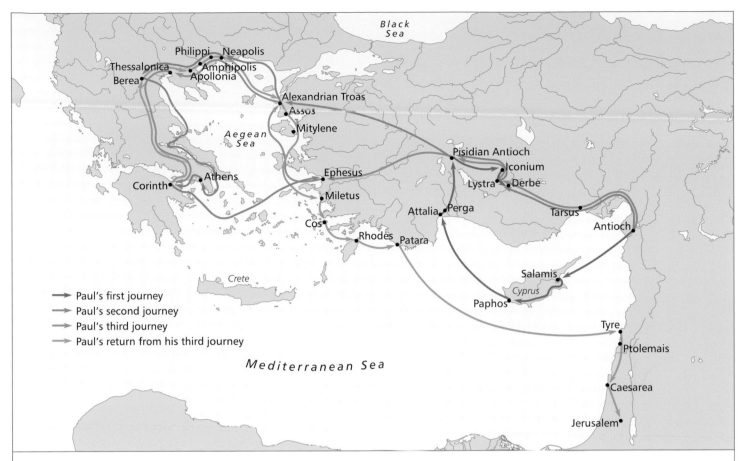

Black Sea

Philippi Neapolis
Thessalonica Amphipolis
Berea Apollonia
Alexandrian Troas
Assos
Aegean Sea Mitylene
Pisidian Antioch
Ephesus Iconium
Athens Lystra Derbe
Corinth Miletus
Attalia Perga Tarsus
Cos Antioch
Rhodes Patara
Salamis
Cyprus
Paphos
Crete
Tyre
Ptolemais
Mediterranean Sea Caesarea
Jerusalem

→ Paul's first journey
→ Paul's second journey
→ Paul's third journey
→ Paul's return from his third journey

PAUL'S TRAVELS

Paul's first journey to spread the news about Jesus began in the town of Antioch, where he was part of the church. As Paul originally came from Tarsus, such a journey would not seem extraordinary. On his second journey, Paul went further west. On his third journey, he revisited many places from his earlier travels.

The letter writer

Paul had received an excellent education as a young man. As he travelled from place to place, he stayed in touch with Christian churches by sending letters: words of advice, rebuke, and encouragement. These letters were treasured in their day. Several of the books of the Bible are letters written by Paul.

Lydia was a wealthy businesswoman in the city of Philippi. She welcomed Paul and believed the message about Jesus. She would have been overjoyed to receive a letter from Paul.

From Paul's letter to the people of Philippi

"Don't worry about anything, but in all your prayers ask God for what you need, always asking him with a thankful heart. And God's peace, which is far beyond human understanding, will keep your hearts and mind safe in union with Christ Jesus.

"My brothers and sisters, fill your minds with those things that are good and that deserve praise: things that are true, noble, right, pure, lovely, and honourable....

"And the God who gives us peace will be with you."
Philippians 4:6–9

CORINTH

One of the places where Paul spent some time was Corinth. It was originally a Greek town in the Roman empire, but when an emperor named Claudius ordered the Jews to leave Rome, some came to Corinth. In the synagogue at Corinth, Paul held discussions about Jesus with Jews and Greeks.

A Jewish couple named Aquila and Priscilla became firm friends of his. They had the same trade as Paul, making tents, and they earned their living in Corinth in this way.

Theatre

Temple

Street entertainers

Temple of Apollo

Cloth merchant

Fine glassware

Butcher's shop

61

CHRISTIANITY IN THE ROMAN EMPIRE

Bread and wine

A church meeting

The churches often met in each other's homes. There, they would have shared bread and wine in the way Jesus had taught at the Last Supper with his disciples. One of Paul's letters describes the ceremony – one that has continued in churches for 2,000 years:

"The Lord Jesus, on the night he was betrayed, took a piece of bread, gave thanks to God, broke it, and said, 'This is my body, which is for you. Do this in memory of me.' In the same way, after the supper he took the cup and said, 'This cup is God's new covenant, sealed with my blood. Whenever you drink it, do so in memory of me.'

"This means that every time you eat this bread and drink from this cup you proclaim the Lord's death until he comes."
1 Corinthians 11:23–26

The church in Puteoli welcomes Paul on his way to Rome. Churches treasured any letters they received from Paul – even copies of ones sent to other churches – so there would have been great delight at meeting the man himself.

P aul's enthusiasm for preaching to the Gentiles was not approved by all. When, after his third great missionary trip, he returned to Jerusalem, his enemies were suspicious. They accused him of taking Gentiles into the part of the Temple reserved for Jews. He was put on trial but saw the episode as an opportunity: he asked to be sent to the emperor's court in Rome.

Paul was sent to Rome on a grain ship that was also carrying other people bound for trial. They started out from Caesarea at the end of the summer sailing season. The weather got worse during the voyage and they were shipwrecked off Malta. Here, once more, Paul preached about Jesus.

In the spring he set off for Rome. There, Paul was greeted by Christians he had never met: they were part of the many new churches that were springing up all over the empire as the apostles carried out the great commission.

However, they faced discouragement too. In the early days, many of Jesus' followers had believed he would come back to set up his kingdom. That had not happened, and they needed to face up to the idea that their hope did not lie in this world. Worse, the Roman authorities had noticed the growth of Christian communities – churches – and were suspicious. Increasingly, believers risked imprisonment and execution.

It was at this time that a Christian named John produced an extraordinary piece of writing from where he was on the prison island of Patmos. This message, which is included in the Bible as the book of Revelation, was a message of hope to inspire Christians everywhere to trust in God and in Jesus' message of God's kingdom: that those who believed in him would be safe in heaven for ever.

His words bring the Bible to a close. The book that began with stories telling of the beginning of time itself, and that tells the history of a nation over more than a thousand years, ends with a glimpse of eternity.

A vision of heaven

On the prison island of Patmos, John, the writer of the book of Revelation, had this vision of heaven:

"I saw a new heaven and a new earth. The first heaven and the first earth disappeared, and the sea vanished. And I saw the Holy City, the new Jerusalem, coming down out of heaven from God, prepared and ready, like a bride dressed to meet her husband. I heard a loud voice speaking from the throne: 'Now God's home is with human beings! He will live with them, and they shall be his people. God himself will be with them, and he will be their God. He will wipe away all tears from their eyes. There will be no more death, no more grief or crying or pain.'"
Revelation 21:1–4

THE SPREAD OF CHRISTIANITY
Many believers helped spread the news about Jesus. When Paul was sent for trial in Rome, he was welcomed by Christians who had learned the faith from other preachers.

Area of Christian communities in 100 CE
Roman empire 117 CE
Paul's journey to Rome

Black Sea

Rome Three Taverns
Forum of Appius
Puteoli
Sicily
Rhegium
Carthage
Syracuse
Patmos
Cnidus
Myra
Crete
Malta
Safe Harbours
Cyprus
Mediterranean Sea
Cyrene
Sidon
Caesarea
Alexandria
Jerusalem

INDEX OF PEOPLE AND PLACE NAMES